PRAYERPY

PRAYERPY

A Prayer Book for
Mental Health Professionals

By Dee M. Sterling, M.A., LCPC

PRAYERPY

CONTENTS

DEDICATION

This book is dedicated to mental health workers, caregivers, and those who remain committed to helping improve the mental and emotional health of others. As a believer in Jesus Christ and licensed clinical professional counselor, it is my desire that those on the frontline of this field have spiritual protection as we encounter the daily traumas of others on a regular basis. It was through that desire that this prayer book was birthed.

The prayers were written with every counselor, psychologist, therapist, social worker, psychiatrist, and the numerous titles in this field, in mind. It is my prayer that it blesses you over and over again, just as it blesses and allows me to complete the work with and for those who need me.

May God continue to give you favor as you soar in this profession!

Dee

DISCLAIMER

This book gives tips based on my own studies, insights and life as a Christian, licensed clinician. It is not meant to replace advice from doctors, therapists, or other experts. Please talk to the right professionals before making big changes to your health, money, or life plans.

During the Reflection of the book, I have tried to recreate events, and/or conversations from my memories of them. In order to maintain their anonymity, I may have changed some identifying characteristics and details such as physical properties, occupations, and places of residence.

The opinions or perspectives shared here are solely mine and do not necessarily reflect the views, policies, or positions of any organization, employer, or affiliated group.

INTRODUCTION

As a young girl, I aspired to become a nurse just like my mother. At 23 years old, I was accepted into a nursing program and attended classes, but I had to drop out of the program due to financial reasons, schedule, and family demands. My life took a different route, and I began working for a financial institution that would later become my career path for 30 plus years. Despite the success, I still felt empty and something inside me wanted to do more. I recall one of my friends saying, "You need to either go back to nursing school or to a counseling program. You help people for free, why not get paid for it?" It was at that moment that I knew that I needed to make a decision. Through prayer, fasting and instructions from God, I believed I had received my answer. During the next weeks, I completed an application for college and two weeks later, I was interviewed for a master's of arts counseling program.

During my time in the counseling program, while raising a family and working a full-time career, I battled so many emotions from feelings of fatigue, stress, and even low self-worth. Those feelings were all challenged in the classes designed for us to deal with our own traumas, but I often still felt overwhelmed. Many of my future colleagues shared the same sentiments, but

———————— ❖ ————————

we kept one another accountable and silently cheered each other on. It was during that time that only prayer and my faith in Jesus kept me going. This gave me the strength to keep showing up for the free clients in internship, cooking for my family, working my full-time job, and staying up late to finish homework assignments. I just wanted to see the end of the program, so I could feel the relief. However, I would soon find out that the real work would begin after I completed my defense for the master's degree and walked the stage.

After graduation, the uncertainties about my purpose continued. I studied for my first level state board exam and passed, but still felt no relief. The work never seemed to cease, as I had more duties to complete over a two-year span post graduation, before I could sit for the second state board exam to become an independent counselor. The work never stopped, so I could never feel a breakthrough or take the time to exhale and bask in my moments of accomplishment. *Had I misheard God? Was I in His timing? Was I a good fit for the profession?* The answers were certain, but what I saw and felt appeared to be the opposite. I learned so much in school, but the real preparation was on the clinical side, in session with real humans with real issues. It was during those times that I had to hold on tightly to my faith to stay the course.

Prayer and a community of close friends and colleagues in the profession were my saving grace. It was during long talks with my support circle and manda-

———————— ❖ ————————

tory supervision meetings that I realized that the feelings I carried were also felt by others. Some were in the same space, while others had surpassed the stages, learned the lessons and moved on, until another situation arose. Many of the prayers were written in my journal, and I often revisited them as part of my daily devotion. Other prayers were spirit-led during times I was unable to write. Other times, colleagues and I would enter the hallways of the school and pray when appropriate. I would not have survived this season of my life without these prayers. I knew then that I had to share these prayers with others.

The topics and prayers listed in this book do not even begin to touch the surface of the many issues we as clinicians encounter on a daily basis, but the ones mentioned were placed on my heart by God. Some of the prayers can be applied to other issues you are facing as well. Through the addition of scriptures after each prayer, it is my personal prayer and hope that the word of God will guide your journey as you navigate the day to day of your professional and personal lives.

PRAYERPY

CHAPTER ONE

GRATITUDE AND THANKSGIVING

PRAYERPY

———————❖———————

———————————— ❖ ————————————

REFLECTION

Being in the mental health profession can be difficult and as helpers, we might not always see or recognize the fruits of our day-to-day labor. It is during these times that we must believe that we are indeed built for this, that we matter, and that we have been equipped professionally, naturally, and spiritually for this profession.

PRAYER

Father God, I thank You for the ability and tenacity to continue the work in this field. I know that it is through You, Christ Jesus, that I have the strength to continue in this fight for and with Your people. When this work becomes hard and overwhelming, I know that I can look to You for my help and protection. Thank You for not allowing the enemy to overtake me or discourage me. You comfort me as I continuously lean into your presence. Thank You for your peace that outweighs all of my human understanding. I thank You for every teacher, supervisor, colleague, and client or patient that I have encountered during my training and career. I ask You to bless each one in a special way for their sacrifice and deposits into my life. I repent for complaining and for feeling unworthy of this role and

———————— ❖ ————————

calling, and I ask You to forgive me. I close all access to the enemy and his suggestions, and I position my-self to hear our voice louder than the enemy, who is only there to kill, steal, and destroy my destiny. Each day, I thank You for another opportunity to help Your people walk in freedom. In Jesus' Name, Amen.

SCRIPTURE

Phillipians 4:13 - I can do all things through Christ who strengthens me.

Psalm 121:1 - I will lift up my eyes to the hills -from whence my help comes.

CHAPTER TWO

THE NEWBIE

PRAYERPY

---------------❖---------------

REFLECTION

Being a new person in the field can look very differ-ent for many people. My classes were filled with future counselors ranging in age from 23-65. Whenever you may have started this journey, it may have felt uncomfortable. Now, you might even realize the slew of responsibilities that you have to juggle in addition to your studies. When I decided to pursue a master's of arts degree in counseling, I worked a full-time career in another field, was a full-time mother of four children ranging from elementary school to college aged, and I also remained very active in my local church. What was I thinking? There was simply not enough time in the day to pursue what God was calling me to do. For those of you who are younger, older, or just beginning, do not give up. I will not lie to you and say that this was an easy journey, because it was very difficult. I cried more than I wanted to and I wanted to give up daily. I made mistakes in and out of sessions and wanted to quit, but God dealt with the perfectionist attitude, and I began to lean on Him for everything that I needed. As I look back at how far I have come and all the clients I have touched, I will tell you that it was well worth the sacrifice.

Whether your story is similar to mine or not, when things start to feel impossible just remember why you

---------------❖---------------

started. Regardless of when you began, remember that you are not alone and each person before you was also a new and felt just as lost and overwhelmed as you do now. We all had to start somewhere. What is important, is that you do not quit.

PRAYER

Dear Lord, I thank You for this new journey. I know that You have given me the strength to persevere through my studies and overcome the stressors of day-to-day activities. Some days it becomes so hard and many days, I allow the enemy to persuade me that I am not in the right field or not good enough, but then You show me that I am right where I need to be. Your thoughts towards me are good and not of evil, and you give me an expected end. Please help me to remain on track and push through my courses, internships, practicums, and exams, while I navigate my daily responsibilities. I will not become weary in well doing because I know I will reap in blessings. I will put all of my trust in You and will not lean on my own understanding, because I know You will show me the path and way to go. In Jesus' Name, Amen.

---- ❖ ----

SCRIPTURE

Galatians 6:9 - Let us not become weary in doing good, for at the proper time we will reap a harvest if we do not give up.

Proverbs 16:3 - Commit to the Lord whatever you do and he will establish your plans,

Jeremiah 29:11 - For I know the thoughts I think towards you, says the Lord, thoughts of peace and not of evil, to give you a future and a hope.

PRAYERPY

---------------- ❖ ----------------

CHAPTER THREE

BOUNDARIES
WORK-LIFE BALANCE

PRAYERPY

———————— ❖ ————————

REFLECTION

The topic of boundaries often comes with many criticisms, but in our profession, it is an act of self-love, courage, and discipline. Healthy boundaries in the field of counseling is necessary to maintain professionalism and define what is acceptable and ethical in the therapeutic relationship. Boundaries can promote trust and foster an environment where the client or patient can heal and grow. Establishing boundaries can easily assist those who suffer from people pleasing behaviors like me. Before entering the master's degree counseling program, I lacked boundaries from every side, whether in my own life or with the lives of others. Even during the earlier years of practicing counseling, I allowed the clients to cross boundaries with me because I lacked confidence and feared that if I did not allow this behavior, I would be unable to maintain clientele. I would allow clients to contact me at any time and even go over their sessions, but when I learned the art and benefits of creating boundaries, I gained respect and confidence. If you are a mental health worker who still struggles with boundaries, my hope is that you find the root cause so that you can heal and monitor how others access you. It will be one of the healthiest choices you make for yourself in this field.

———————— ❖ ————————

PRAYER

Dear Heavenly Father, I thank You for your love towards me. As I receive your love, teach me to see myself just as You see me. Your word reminds me that I am fearfully and wonderfully made. Lord, I repent for not always believing or displaying that in my interactions with others. Today, I choose to walk in confidence and courage as you continue to guide me in both my professional and personal relationships. I will continue to guard my heart in all situations and seek wisdom concerning my clients and those who you have placed in my life. I will obey You as you instruct me on how to navigate what the access to my life should look like. I know that some clients may require more of me during certain times, but I pray that You will not allow me to stumble and fall into dangerous territories or go the wrong way. When I feel weak, I thank You for your strength to continue to do those things that feel hard. When I feel afraid, I thank You for your perfect love that cancels all my fears. Thank You for delivering me from the spirit of people pleasing. Thank You for giving me the courage to stand firm in my decision when my answer is a yes, and to rebuke the enemy of guilt when my answer must be no. In Jesus' Name, Amen.

---- ❖ ----

SCRIPTURE

Psalms 139:14 - I will praise You for I am fearfully and wonderfully made; Marvelous are Your work: and that my soul knows very well.

Proverbs 4:23 - Above all else, guard your heart for everything you do flows from it.

Matthew 5:37 - But let your Yes be Yes and your No, No. For whatever is more than these is from the evil one.

1 John 4:18 - There is no fear in love; but perfect love casts out fear, because fear involves torment. But he who fears has not been made perfect in love.

PRAYERPY

❖

CHAPTER FOUR

WISDOM

PRAYERPY

---------------- ❖ ----------------

REFLECTION

As licensed clinicians, we learn many techniques and theories in our schooling that we can utilize in our sessions. I remember being encouraged to choose one theory that I identified with, but after graduation, I found myself utilizing many techniques and theories as I learned to give each client a tailored experience. There will be times that we need to consult with our peers and overseers because we will not always have the right answers or know the right diagnosis. As humans, we will not always get it right, but I encourage you to lean not only into your book knowledge and resources, but the Lord as well. This will ensure you are doing your very best for those that are in your care.

PRAYER

Dear Lord,

Thank you Lord for a sound mind and the ability to retain knowledge, but most importantly, I thank You for your wisdom. I thank You that the word reminds me that wisdom is the principle thing and I also must have understanding. Lord, this field can be uncertain and hard at times, and many days I do not know if I am making the right decisions regarding those You have placed in my care, but I thank You for your favor and grace towards me. I thank You for the wise counsel of practitioners and prayer warriors that You have placed

———————— ❖ ————————

around me to help me when I become unsure. Lord, I thank You for the victory I receive, just by being in the presence of these wise ones. I decree continued blessings of victory over my life as I continue to work in humility with those You assigned to help me in the profession. I thank You that wherever I go in the profession, I will always remain teachable, and that the spirit of pride and arrogance will not overtake me. I decree over my life that as I walk in humility, favor and wisdom will follow. In Jesus' Name, Amen.

SCRIPTURE

Proverbs 4:7 - Wisdom is the principal thing; Therefore get wisdom. And in all your getting, get understanding.

Proverbs 24:6 - For by wise counsel you will wage your own war, And in a multitude of counselors there is safety.

James 4:6 - But He gives more grace. Therefore He says: God resists the proud, But gives grace to the humble.

Proverbs 11:2 - When pride comes, then comes shame; But with the humble is wisdom.

CHAPTER FIVE

IMPOSTER SYNDROME / COMPARISON

PRAYERPY

———————— ❖ ————————

REFLECTION

Imposter syndrome can be characterized by an increase in levels of self-doubt and negative self-perception. A person suffering from imposter syndrome tends to attribute their successes and self-worth to external factors like luck, random chance or good will. This negative belief can often lead to acts of perfectionism, people pleasing, or comparison.

Prior to entering the field of counseling, I struggled with having a negative self-image. I held the belief that someone else could always do anything better than I could. This often left me stuck in negative thought patterns, or comparing myself to someone else. The negative thoughts often caused me to remain immobile, meaning I would often not do anything with hopes that someone else would come along and do it better. The truth of the matter is that there will always be someone who can do things better than you or I can, but we bring a very important component to the mix. We bring our own personalities, creativities, expertise, ideas, and God-given talents to the table. A pastor once told me, "Dee, you are waiting for God to send someone else to do what He told you to do, but there is no one else who has what He gave you." Those words will always ring in my ear and they often jolt me back into position when I am tempted to hide.

There is enough room for everyone to succeed. Despite the number of mental health professionals in the

—————————— ❖ ——————————

world, there will always be the clients or patients that will be drawn to you because you will have the keys to help them unlock the potential inside. If you are busy being another person or comparing yourself to your role model, your clients will never receive what they need. Be authentic and love who God made you to be. It is in your authenticity that you will succeed in every area of your life.

PRAYER

Dear Father God,

Thank you for Your patience and your kindness towards me. Even when I did not see myself the way you created me, you took Your time with me, guided me in scripture and purpose, and sent those to lift me up. You created me in your likeness and image, and I know that I was chosen to do good works, which You already prepared me to do. When the enemy comes to kill, steal, and destroy my peace and purpose through comparison, I resist him and he flees. I repent for comparing myself to another person, and I ask You to remove any envy, doubt, and confusion from my heart. Today I decree that my joy and peace have been restored. As I lean into Your thoughts and plans for me, which are good and not of evil, I am being transformed daily by the renewing of my mind. In Jesus' Name, Amen.

❖

SCRIPTURE

Ephesians 2:10 - For we are His workmanship, created in Christ Jesus for good works, which God prepared beforehand that we should walk in them.

Jeremiah 29:11 - For I know the thoughts I think towards you, says the Lord, thoughts of peace and not of evil, to give you a future and a hope.

Romans 12:2 - And do not be conformed to this world, but be transformed by the renewing of your mind, that you may prove what is that good and acceptable and perfect will of God.

PRAYERPY

---------- ❖ ----------

CHAPTER SIX

BURNOUT /
COMPASSION FATIGUE

PRAYERPY

———————❖———————

❖

REFLECTION

As a helper in any helping profession, one might experience what is referred to as burnout or compassion fatigue. They are often used interchangeably, but they are quite different. Burnout is a term referring to the general exhaustion and lack of interest or motivation regarding one's work in the field. Compassion fatigue, also called vicarious trauma, refers to the negative emotions that many mental health workers might feel from the intense desire to help relieve the suffering of their clients. Although different in meaning, those who suffer from either, can be impacted by negative physical, mental, and behavioral symptoms.

I can recall many evenings having feelings of mild depression, exhaustion, frustration, and lack of motivation. I felt hopeless and detached from the very clients that I wanted to help so badly. I often felt as if I lacked the abilities to continue the work that I once loved so much. Additionally, I had physical symptoms such as headaches and insomnia, but I never made the correlation with the work of counseling.

Some of the feelings described can sometimes lead to shame for most professionals and can cause many of us to suffer in silence. It is imperative that we engage in community with other counselors. It is also our responsibility to ourselves and the clients we help, to prioritize both our physical and mental health well-being. If we fail to do so, we will operate on autopilot

———————— ❖ ————————

from an empty cup and become less effective in the work we do. It is my prayer that every mental health worker from the front desk to the hospital attendant, would not only recognize the symptoms of burnout or compassion fatigue, but also learn the spiritual and natural ways to fight against it.

PRAYER

Dear Lord, I thank You for the ability to continue in this profession when my body feels weak and I want to give up. When I am weary and burdened with the cares of the world and the load of my clients' issues, I thank You for giving me peace. I pray that Your peace transcends all negativity and every evil thing that comes along to try to destroy my peace. I decree and declare that no weapon formed against me will prosper. I have a sound mind and my body is in good emotional, physical, mental and spiritual health, just as my soul prospers. In Jesus' Name, Amen.

SCRIPTURE

Matthew 11:28 - Come to Me, all you who labor and are heavy laden, and I will give you rest.

CHAPTER SEVEN

STRESS

PRAYERPY

---- ❖ ----

REFLECTION

Being in the helping profession can be both emotionally and physically overwhelming. If you are reading this as a student, intern, or clinician trying to accumulate more hours for licensure, or even studying for the state boards, this section is for you. If you are working in a private practice or an overcrowded inpatient facility, this section is for you. If you are a parent, husband or wife, full-time employee working in another field, and also carrying a full caseload of clients, this section is also for you. If you are the professor who teaches and supervises practicum students, while also running your own practice, this section is for you too. Due to the high demands of those needing help, the list of scenarios for those in this field can vary.

I highly recommend that every person in this field find a therapist, as stress can manifest in our bodies in different ways. Many of us have learned to carry the weight and problems of others, while still fulfilling our personal responsibilities, and the signs can be easy to ignore. During my time in school, I worked a full-time job, raised four children, worked at a private practice on the weekends to accumulate internship hours, wrote papers, and also studied for exams. Not only did I cry daily, but my stress levels were so high that I could not even remember eating a plate of food, or even driving to the train for work. Stress took me to the point of auto-pilot, which can have negative effects on the body and behaviors. Do not allow this work to stress you to the point that you begin to dislike the good that you are doing.

———————— ❖ ————————

We are needed, but not to the point that we ignore ourselves.

Take a breath, see a therapist and/or medical doctor, and pray.

PRAYER

Dear Lord,

Thank You for your comfort and peace that helps me get through the cares of life. Lord, there are times when the pressures of this profession try to cause stress and weariness in my heart, but Your word reminds me that I can come to You and lay my cares onto You, and You will give me rest. It is only You who can lighten this load that is trying to bring stress upon my body and mind.

Lord, I ask that You cover my thoughts and decisions and that You guide me in all your ways. I know that I can do all things through You, Jesus. Therefore, I repent for not inviting You in and trying to do it all by myself. Teach me to seek your face and to sit in your presence when I have too much on my plate. My hope is in You and I know that You will not allow me to grow weary or give up. As I wait on You to instruct me, I thank You for renewing my strength to move ahead. In Jesus' Name, Amen.

---------------- ❖ ----------------

SCRIPTURE

John 14:27 - Peace I leave with you, My peace I give to you; not as the world gives do I give to you. Let not your heart be troubled, neither let it be afraid.

Matthew 11:28-30 - Come to Me, all you who labor and are heavy laden, and I will give you rest. 29 Take My yoke upon you and learn from Me, for I am [a]gentle and lowly in heart, and you will find rest for your souls. 30 For My yoke is easy and My burden is light.

Isaiah 40:31 - But those who wait on the LORD Shall renew their strength; They shall mount up with wings like eagles, They shall run and not be weary, They shall walk and not faint.

PRAYERPY

CHAPTER EIGHT

ANXIETY

PRAYERPY

---------------❖---------------

————————— ❖ —————————

REFLECTION

As a clinician, one of the many symptoms I observe the most in clients is anxiety. Whether diagnosed or simply feeling overwhelmed with life issues, anxiety is a real experience for both the clients and many professionals. From a psychological perspective, anxiety is the feeling of worry or nervousness that typically occurs in the absence of an imminent threat. Although it has been compared to fear, it differs from fear because fear pertains to the body's natural response to immediate danger.

About 20 years ago, I was diagnosed with a heart issue. Since then, I have had surgery and been healed with no other symptoms. Praise God! Yet during the time prior to and after the diagnosis, I suffered from anxiety. I lived with the anxiety of becoming ill again, being in public and having an emergency situation, and the list goes on. My licensed therapist at that time walked me through various techniques to help me conquer the anxiety that was attempting to cripple my entire life. It tried to halt my day-to-day coming and going, my interactions at work, and my future profession in counseling. Anytime I anticipated something *possibly* going wrong, I would feel anxiety trying to rear its ugly head, but thank God for Jesus and clinical remedies to help me to refocus. I say this because each time I meet a new client or am faced with something I have never handled before in this field, anxiety attempts to creep in. Is there imminent danger? No! However, the mind can create scenarios that can possibly limit your professional potential. Perhaps you can

———————— ❖ ————————

relate to this or know someone who can. If so, seek out your own professional and medical care to ensure you are pouring from a full and healthy cup, not an empty one. We are humans too and must take the necessary steps to ensure our wellness, not just the wellness of others.

PRAYER

Father God,

Thank You for keeping me during times of uncertainty. I admit that I have often yielded to the thoughts and fears that life has thrown at me. I repent for not always placing You above those thoughts and circumstances. I repent for pouring from an empty cup and relying on my own strength to get me through, but today I ask for You to help me. I surrender my thoughts, my fears, my circumstances, my clients, and all my worries to You. I know without a shadow of a doubt that nothing is too hard for You and that You will never allow the enemy to sift me, shake me, or break me down. My cup runs over today with confidence and the assurance that my future is set and in your hands. Even when the enemy comes to distract, dismay, and taunt me with the anxiety and the cares of this world, You raise up a standard against his schemes. Today, I give all my cares, worries, anxieties and burdens to You because I know You care for me and about everything that concerns me. In Jesus' Name, Amen.

❖

SCRIPTURE

Psalms 23:5 - You prepare a table before me in the presence of my enemies;You anoint my head with oil; My cup runs over.

Isaiah 59:19 - So shall they fear The name of the LORD from the west, And His glory from the rising of the sun; When the enemy comes in like a flood, The Spirit of the LORD will lift up a standard against him.

1 Peter 5:7 - Casting all your care upon Him, for He cares for you.

PRAYERPY

CHAPTER NINE

FINANCES

PRAYERPY

---------------❖---------------

❖

REFLECTION

Just as the ages and background can vary in this field, everyone's financial situation will look differently as well. I attended classes and internships with those who did not have financial obligations, others who had families, and some who had to temporarily quit jobs to complete the program and hours for graduation and state licensure. Please ensure that you have prayed about your particular situation and have prepared ahead of time for what may lie ahead. Be wise and realistic about your finances and your goals.

If you are a new clinician who has changed careers, or a student unable to work due to internship, please be encouraged through this temporary phase. Trust me, this will all pay off soon. Truthfully, there are many hats that one can wear in the field and the finances are there to make, if you are interested. Many clinicians own businesses, work in hospitals or within the court system, many teach or do public speaking all over the world, many write books, perform research studies, and the list continues depending on the field of study and level of degree obtained.

PRAYER

Thank You Lord for giving me the power to gain wealth. I love what I do, but sometimes I do not always see the fruits of my labor. Lord, I ask You for divine

——————————— ❖ ———————————

strategy and discipline in business and in my finances. Lord, thank you for sustaining me financially in this field and continuing to give me the creative abilities to go far and beyond what I ever imagined. Thank You for ordering my steps on this career path. Lord, Your word reminds me that your blessings make me rich and that there is no sorrow, so thank You for the provision and the increase. I decree that I have all my needs met and that You provide me with the wisdom on how to do everything that You have instructed. In Jesus' Name Amen.

SCRIPTURE

Deuteronomy 8:18 - And you shall remember the LORD your God, for it is He who gives you power to get wealth, that He may establish His covenant which He swore to your fathers, as it is this day.

Proverbs 10:22 - The blessing of the LORD makes one rich, and He adds no sorrow with it.

CHAPTER TEN

TRANSFERENCE / COUNTERTRANSFERENCE

PRAYERPY

❖

REFLECTION

Transference and countertransference are one of the first topics we learned and were warned about in our therapeutic relationships with our clients and/or patients. Transference is when the client transfers an unconscious feeling, desire, or expectation from another person toward the clinician. On the other hand, countertransference is the reverse of transference, which is about the clinician's emotional reaction or expectation towards the client. As a clinician, it is highly likely that you will experience one or the other with a client or two, but do not be too hard on yourself. Experiencing countertransference as a clinician simply means you are human. Humans make mistakes and get right back up and try again. The great thing about our profession is that we are provided with so many resources, along with other professionals who can guide us when we face these challenges or go astray. The good thing to know is that we can utilize a client's transference towards us as a way to get to know them better, as we assist them in these feelings.

Countertransference can occur in different ways, and it is the responsibility of every clinician to not do any harm to the client by continuing therapy without correcting these behaviors.

As a young clinician, I loved everyone and I remember feeling a strong concern for one of my clients as I would my own child. I immediately recognized

——————— ❖ ———————

my feelings of protection which were outside of the scope of the profession, and I discussed and cried about it in supervision. I was provided a safe place to express myself and learned techniques to help me learn boundaries and deal with my own traumas from childhood. Your experiences may be different, such as feeling dreadful about a particular session or client, or overidentifying with the client's story that limits your professional insight and ability to assist them. Whatever the case may be, do not ignore the signs or think this cannot be turned around. On the other side of this, there can be so much growth and healing in both your personal and professional life.

PRAYER

Father God,

Thank You for Your protection and for always providing me with a way of escape. Even when I make a mistake, Your wisdom guides me back to where I need to be. Lord, Your word reminds me that there is safety in the midst of wisdom and wise counsel. Thank You for surrounding me with those in the profession that I can trust to correct and steer me back. Thank You for revealing to me where I still need healing or just a change in my perspectives. I repent for anything that may have unknowingly caused harm or an offense to a client. I also forgive any clients who may have offended me or had false expectations of me due to trau-

❖

mas from his or her past. Thank You Lord for freedom, growth, and perseverance. In Jesus' Name, Amen.

SCRIPTURE

1 Corinthians 10:13 - No temptation has overtaken you except such as is common to man; but God is faithful, who will not allow you to be tempted beyond what you are able, but with the temptation will also make the way of escape, that you may be able to bear it.

Proverbs 11:14 - Where there is no counsel, the people fall; But in the multitude of counselors there is safety.

PRAYERPY

---------------- ❖ ----------------

CHAPTER ELEVEN

EXPERIENCING VIOLENCE / FEAR

PRAYERPY

❖

REFLECTION

The clients or patients that we see can be very un-predictable. Many people are hurting all over the world and pain can manifest in different ways for many people. Some react to pain and confusion in violence, and others might react in a less aggressive manner.. Despite the training and precautions we take, things can still happen. My job is not to alarm you, but prepare you for situations whether you are in a private practice, hospital setting, or outpatient facility. For example, those of you who work in hospitals might have to restrain patients from self-harming. Get to know your clients and patients and use your best judgement when engaging.

As a clinician, I have not personally experienced any physical violence with any clients, but many of my colleagues have experienced threats and stalking. I did have an encounter with a new client who was verbally intimidating in session. The client immediately regained composure, and it was later revealed that she was previously diagnosed at another facility with Borderline Personality Disorder.

It is important to ensure that as we are working later hours due to our clients 9-5 work schedules, we pay attention to the warning signs. For the clinician who works in an inpatient facility or the addiction recovery center, it is important to remain watchful of your surroundings. Many patients or clients that you may

❖

encounter can suffer from severe mental health challenges or substance abuse. Therefore, it is our duty to know our clients and ensure safety precautions at all times.

PRAYER

Dear Lord,

I thank You and praise You for being my protector, my refuge, and safety in the time of trouble. Thank You for hiding me from the seen and unseen dangers around me. As I do Your will and work in this profession, I ask for wisdom and discernment in how I engage with those who might have mental health challenges, anger, resentment, or who simply feel lost and abandoned in this world. You promised me that You would never leave me or forsake me. I pray for the hearts of those who do not know You, and I pray that they always see and feel Your presence when they encounter me in a session or just in passing. You have not given me the spirit of fear, but of power, love, and a sound mind. I decree that no weapon formed against my life or those of my clients will prosper. Thank You for giving your angels charge over me to keep me from hurt, harm, and danger. Thank You Jesus, Amen.

---- ❖ ----

SCRIPTURE

Psalm 46:1 - God is our refuge and strength, A very present help in trouble

*Deuteronomy 31:6 - Be strong and of good courage, do not fear nor be afraid of them; for the L*ORD *your God, He is the One who goes with you. He will not leave you nor forsake you*

Psalm 91:11 - For He shall give His angels charge over you, To keep you in all your ways.

PRAYERPY

CHAPTER TWELVE

SURVIVING SUICIDE
OR
THE SUICIDAL CLIENT

PRAYERPY

———————— ❖ ————————

REFLECTION

In the master's degree program I attended, once a student reached a certain level in the program, students would begin practicum. Practicum provided future clinician students with the opportunity to "practice" in the field with real life clients with real life issues. This took place in school, in a counseling room, with an emergency phone to connect with the professor or campus police, and under strict supervision. Clients who registered with the university's counseling department were assigned to a student. They also signed a liability waiver and were aware that we were students in training, but under strict supervision of a licensed professional. To my surprise, my very first client was suicidal. I had learned all the signs and assessment strategies in the classroom, but felt afraid, unsure, and definitely unprepared for the role of a counselor at that moment. After my assessment with the client, it was confirmed that my client fit the full criteria of someone who planned to commit suicide. I knew I could not cry at that moment because critical steps needed to be taken. Instead, I prayed silent prayers in my mind and called my professor who immediately came to assist. As the professor, a licensed counselor, re-assessed the client, it was agreed that the client would be transported to a behavioral health hospital or in-patient facility.

As we waited for the ambulance to arrive at the school, my faith was waning and I could hear the enemy whisper that I was not fit to be in this field. At one point, I remember agreeing. Once the ambulance took my very first client

———————— ❖ ————————

away, I began to cry uncontrollably while my professor held me until the sobs diminished. It was at that moment that I needed the Lord's intervention to remain on this journey of helping others. My professor did everything to ensure that my client was transported to a facility, met the family, and gave me a courtesy call to let me know that there was nothing else I could do at that point and that I had done a very good job. Since that was our first visit and I was under school guidelines, I could not reach out to the client. As of today, I have no idea if that person is still alive as they never reached out again and no longer fit the criteria to be seen by a student counselor. I have seen many similar clients since that time and each one tugs at my heart in a different capacity, but the Lord's wisdom and strength always provides me with the tools I need to succeed.

PRAYER

Dear Lord,

Thank You for my experience in the field and for keeping my mind calm during times of chaos and uncertainty. When I lose all hope and confidence, You always promise to never leave me or forsake me. Your perfect love casts out all my fears and anxiety. When I lean into You, You always show yourself strong as my refuge and my strength in the time of trouble. Thank You for protecting me and the clients that I serve. Continue to saturate the counseling rooms I sit in with your presence and anointing. May Your presence be so strong that those who enter troubled, feel the peace that

❖

passes all human understanding. Although I am trained to follow all the steps to keep my clients safe and help them cope, I ask You, Father, to intervene and guide me every step of the way. In Jesus' Name, Amen.

SCRIPTURE

Deuteronomy 31:6 - Be strong and of good courage, do not fear nor be afraid of them; for the LORD your God, He is the One who goes with you. He will not leave you nor forsake you.

Psalm 46:1 - God is our refuge and strength, a very present help in trouble.

PRAYERPY

www.ingramcontent.com/pod-product-compliance
Lightning Source LLC
Chambersburg PA
CBHW072048040426
42447CB00012BB/3069